# puzzles & games

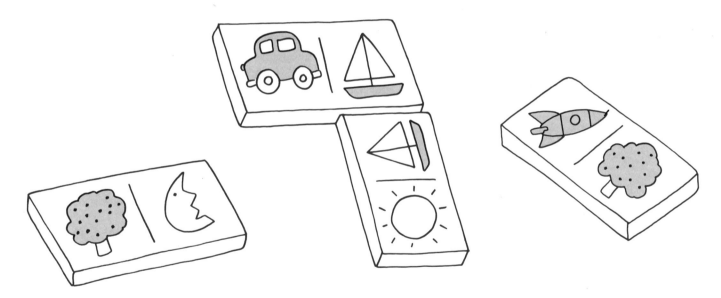

Developed by Macmillan Educational Company
Written by Virginia Satkowski
Text illustrated by Patricia Schories
Cover illustrated by Patrick Girouard

Newbridge Educational Programs

Published in 1995 by Newbridge Communications, Inc., a K-III Education Co., New York.

# TABLE OF CONTENTS

# TABLE OF CONTENTS
## Continued

**You need:** scissors
magazines with colorful
   pictures
glue
9″ × 12″ oaktag
record or tape player
record or tape of lively music

**Steps:**

1. Cut out large, colorful pictures from magazines, enough for half the children in your class.

2. Glue each picture onto a 9″ × 12″ piece of oaktag; then cut it in half.

3. Ask the children to stand in a circle. Shuffle the picture halves and give one half to each child. If there is an odd number of children in your class, choose one child to help you start and stop the music.

4. Play lively music on a record or tape player. As the music plays, children will skip or walk counterclockwise in a circle.

5. When you stop the music, the children must match picture halves. They then may trade for different halves and play the game again.

**Variations:**

1. Make this a shape- and color-matching activity. Cut a variety of shapes from construction paper of various colors, making each shape a different color. Glue each shape to the center of a piece of oaktag and cut it in half to create two puzzle pieces. Each child gets a puzzle piece. When the music stops, children must match up their puzzle pieces by shape and color.

2. To make this an Easter game, cut several large egg shapes from oaktag. Decorate each shape with colorful zigzags, stripes, polka dots, and so on, using crayons or markers. Cut the eggs in half, varying the cut on each egg. Then give each child half an egg. When the music stops, children will match their halves.

# LEADER, MAY I?
## Listening Game

**You need:** chalk

### Steps:

1. Groups of eight to ten children may play this game. On the playground, draw two parallel chalk lines, about 12' apart and 10' long.

2. Choose one child to be the leader and have him or her stand behind one line. Ask the other players to line up along the other line, facing the leader.

3. The leader says the name of the first player on the right and gives him or her a movement instruction—for example, "Nancy, take three steps forward on tiptoe." The player named must ask, "Leader, may I?" before following the instruction.

4. The leader continues to give a movement instruction to each player in turn, such as, "Take two giant steps," "Hop forward three times," "Jump forward once." If a player does not ask, "Leader, may I?" before following the instruction, he or she remains at or returns to the starting line.

5. The first player to cross the line that the leader is standing behind wins the round and becomes the leader for the next round. The former leader joins the other players on the opposite line.

### Variation:

Instead of giving movement instructions, the leader may clap out a simple rhythm with his or her hands for the players to repeat, one at a time—for example, "clap-clap-pause-clap," "clap-pause-clap-pause-clap," "clap-pause-clap," "clap-clap-clap." If the player repeats the series of claps correctly, he or she may take one giant step forward. If not, the player remains where he or she is, and the next player takes a turn. The first player to cross the line that the leader is standing behind wins the round and becomes the new leader.

### Steps:

1. Divide the class into pairs of children and have the pairs spread out in an open area of the classroom. If you have an uneven number of children in your class, let one child be your partner.

2. Call out simple instructions, one at a time, for children to follow. Some examples: "Touch your forehead to your partner's forehead." "Touch right hands with your partner." "Touch your knees to your partner's knees." "Put your hands on your partner's shoulders." "Touch backs with your partner." "Touch your toes to your partner's toes." Pause a few seconds between each instruction to give children time to get in position.

3. Partners will do each action, holding the position until the next instruction is given. However, if you call out, "Stick like glue!" after an instruction, children must hold that position as they follow subsequent instructions. When it becomes too difficult for children to maneuver, call out, "Come unstuck!"

4. If partners do not follow the instructions given or if they come unstuck before you tell them to, they become "stuck in the pot of glue" and must sit down. Continue playing the game until only three or four pairs of children are left.

### Variations:

1. Make this game more challenging for older children by instructing them to move when they are "sticking like glue"—for example, "Take three steps backward." "Hop two times." "Turn around in a circle." "Kneel."

2. Have two or three pairs of children stand in front of the class. Call out instructions for the pairs to follow. When a pair becomes unstuck or does not follow the instructions, that pair is out. Continue until only one pair of children remains. Then select another two or three pairs of children to follow more instructions, making sure each child has a turn.

## WEB OF FRIENDS

**You need:** a ball of yarn

**Steps:**

1. Ask children to stand in a wide circle. Give one child the ball of yarn.

2. He or she calls out a classmate's name and throws or rolls the ball of yarn to that child, keeping the end of the yarn in his or her hand.

3. The child whose name is called must catch the ball of yarn and then wrap the yarn loosely around a part of his or her body (e.g., the waist, a leg, a foot, or an arm). Then that child calls another child's name and throws or rolls the ball of yarn to him or her. The game continues until all the children are woven together. If a child doesn't catch the ball of yarn, the teacher or another child may pick it up and pass it to the child whose name was called.

## "WHO" CLUES

**Steps:**

1. Divide the class into two teams. Have the teams form two lines facing each other, about 5' apart. Give the teams about three minutes to study the clothing and features of the children on the opposite team.

2. Next, ask the two teams to sit on the floor with their backs to each other.

3. The first child on one team becomes the clue-giver. Select a child from the other team to be the "who." Both these children stand in front of their teams, facing their teammates and each other.

4. The clue-giver gives his or her team three clues describing the child who is the "who." The clue-giver may name the "who"'s hair color, eye color, kind of shirt or other clothing. The children on the clue-giver's team have three guesses to name the child being described. If they guess correctly, their team gets a point.

5. The clue-giver sits down. The "who" now becomes the clue-giver for his or her team, and a new "who" is selected from the first team. The game continues until all the children have had turns as both "who" and as clue-giver. The team with the most points wins.

# RING PASS
## Relay Game

**You need:** metal or plastic rings—the centers from rolls of tape; curtain rings; large washers; children's toys—three for each team

### Steps:

1. Divide your class into three or four equal teams. Have the teams line up in single files.

2. Place three metal or plastic rings on the floor in front of the first player on each team.

3. When the starting signal is given, the first player on each team picks up one ring, slips it onto an index finger, and then passes it to the next player by extending the index finger and sliding it onto that child's extended index finger.

4. The first player next picks up the second ring and passes it along in the same manner, then does the same with the third ring.

5. The rings are passed down the rows in this way. If a ring is dropped, the last player to touch it must pick it up, put it back on his or her finger, and continue passing it. When the last child on each team receives a ring, he or she slides it off the index finger and onto the floor. When a team's three rings are on the floor by the last player, the team sits down. The first team to sit down is the winner.

**Variations:**

1. Instead of using their fingers, older children may use plastic straws or thin wooden sticks to pass the rings.

2. Ask children to sit in a large circle on the floor. Give every other child a ring. Call out an instruction—for example, "Pass rings to the right." Children follow your instructions, passing the rings from index finger to index finger, until you call out another instruction. Change instructions frequently so that children must react quickly to the instructions. Any player who drops a ring keeps it and leaves the circle. The game is over when there are no more rings to pass or when only three or four children remain.

# PEBBLE PLUNK
## Relay Game

**You need:** two or three empty plastic
margarine tubs
two or three buckets
water
masking tape
pebbles (two for each child)

**Steps:**

1. Divide your class into two or three equal teams.

2. Place an empty plastic margarine tub in a bucket and fill the bucket with about 8″ of water. Prepare one bucket for each team.

3. Set the buckets in a row, about 4′ apart. Then place a 12″ strip of masking tape about 8″ in front of each bucket.

4. Place a long strip of masking tape on the floor, about 5′ in front of the row of buckets and parallel to it.

5. Ask each team to line up behind the long strip of masking tape, opposite a bucket.

6. Give each child two pebbles. At the starting signal, the first player on each team runs to the team's bucket and stands behind the short strip of tape. The player drops his or her two pebbles into the bucket from shoulder height, trying to drop them into the margarine tub. The players then tag the next players on their teams and go to the end of their teams' lines.

7. When all the players have taken their turns, count the pebbles in each team's margarine tub. The team that dropped the most pebbles into the margarine tub is the winner.

**Variation:**

Place a plastic poker chip or large button on the bottom of each bucket in about 8″ of water. Give each child two pennies. The players on each team drop their pennies into the buckets, trying to cover the poker chip or button. The team that covers the chip or button completely or most completely is the winner.

# FLOATING CARDS
## Classroom Game

**You need:** deck of playing cards
three or four small pails
masking tape

### Steps:

1. Remove the kings, queens, and jacks from the deck of cards. Separate the remaining cards into suits and set them aside.

2. Set one pail on the floor, and ask a child to come forward. Give the child a face card. Ask him or her to grip a short end with thumb and index finger. Dangling the card perpendicular to the floor, the child should let the card drop from shoulder height toward the pail. The card should flutter away to one side.

3. Next, ask the child to hold the card facedown and parallel to the floor, with the thumb on top and the index finger on the bottom. Have the child hold the card in this way at shoulder height over the pail and drop it. The card should float straight down into the pail.

4. Let each child take a few practice turns using the face cards, dropping them into a pail as described in step 3. After children have practiced for a few minutes, collect the face cards and set them aside.

5. Divide the class into three or four equal teams and give each team a set of ten cards of one suit, from ace to ten. The teams distribute the cards among themselves so that each child has at least one card. Some children may have two cards.

6. Set three or four pails in a row on the floor, about 5' apart. Place two long strips of masking tape on the floor, one parallel to and 12" in front of the pails, and the other parallel to and about 6' in front of the pails.

7. The teams line up in single files behind the masking tape farthest from the pails. One at a time, the child at the front of each line runs to the strip of tape nearest the team's pail. Players try to drop their cards into the pails, holding the cards as they did when they practiced. Each child then goes to the end of his or her team's line.

8. When all the cards have been dropped, count how many are in each team's pail. The team with the most cards in its pail wins.

### Variation:

Pairs of children may play a simpler version of this game. Give one child ten red cards and the other ten black cards. Have them alternate turns dropping cards one at a time into a pail. The child who gets the most cards in the pail is the winner.

# ELEPHANT IN A BAG
## Listening Game

**You need:** brown-paper grocery bag with the top folded over and stapled closed

ELEPHANT!

**Steps:**

1. Have the class stand in a circle.

2. Give one child the closed brown-paper grocery bag.

3. Play the part of the caller, to begin the game. The caller stands in the center of the circle and calls out the name of a heavy or light object that is supposedly in the grocery bag—such as an elephant, baby bird, lots of bricks, pencil, balloon, huge rock, television set, pillow, butterfly, airplane.

4. The child with the grocery bag must pretend that the bag is very heavy or very light, depending on what the caller says is in the bag. The child passes the bag to the player on his or her left, who continues to pantomime. The bag is passed clockwise around the circle, and each child pantomimes how light or heavy the bag is.

5. After a short time as caller, select a child to replace you in the center of the circle. Change callers periodically during the game.

6. The caller may change the contents of the bag at any time by naming another object. The children then pantomime the bag's weight as if it held the new object.

7. If a child pantomimes incorrectly (e.g., a child pretends to struggle as he or she lifts the bag when it is supposed to be holding a feather), he or she must imitate an elephant for a few seconds. Continue the game for as long as it holds children's interest.

## DOG-BONE RELAY

**You need:** dog-bone pattern
scissors
pencil
oaktag

**Steps:**

1. Reproduce the dog-bone pattern on this page and cut it out. Trace the pattern three or four times onto oaktag. Then cut out the dog bones.

2. Divide the class into three or four equal teams. Have each team line up in single file.

3. Write the following words on the chalkboard: *over, under, around,* and *on.*

4. The object of the relay is to pass the dog bone down each team's line four times. The first time, each player passes the bone *over* the head to the child behind him or her. On the next lap of the relay, each child passes it *under* the right leg. Then each child passes it *around* his or her back. Finally, each child holds the dog bone *on* his or her head, until the child next in line takes it. You may have one team demonstrate how to pass the dog bone on each lap of the relay.

5. At the start of the relay, the first player on each team passes the bone *over* his or her head to the next person, and so on down the line. When the dog bone reaches the last child in line, he or she runs to the front of the team to begin the second lap by passing the dog bone *under* his or her right leg.

6. The team that completes all four laps of the relay first is the winner.

## ALPHABET TAG

**Steps:**

1. Choose one child to be *It.* Ask the other children to stand in a circle. The child who is *It* stands outside the circle.

2. *It* names any letter of the alphabet. One child in the circle starts calling out the alphabet beginning with *A.* The child standing to the left of the first child calls out *B,* the next child *C,* and so on around the circle until the letter named by *It* is called.

3. The child who calls out that letter becomes the chaser, running clockwise around the circle trying to tag *It* before *It* reaches the spot where the chaser was standing. If the child tags *It,* the chaser returns to his or her place in the circle. If the child does not tag *It,* he or she becomes *It* for the next round.

**Variation:**

This game may be played with numbers instead of letters. Older children may select numbers higher than the number of children in the circle.

**Steps:**

1. Play this game on the playground. Divide your class into groups of eight to ten children each.

2. Have the children in each group form a "snake" by lining up in single file and placing their hands on the shoulders of the child in front of them.

3. The child at the front of the line is the snake's head; the child at the end is the snake's tail.

4. When the starting signal is given, the child who is the snake's head begins to run, with the other children in the snake keeping their hands on the shoulders of the person in front of them and running along behind the snake's head. The child who is the snake's head must try to tag the child who is the snake's tail.

5. If the children forming the snake break the formation during the game, they must stop and quickly get back into position before continuing. When the snake's head tags the snake's tail, the child who is the snake's head goes to the end of the snake, places his or her hands on the shoulders of the last child, and becomes the new tail. The child who was second now becomes the snake's head, and the game is repeated.

6. Play the game until each child has had a turn to be the snake's head. If a child playing the snake's head cannot tag the tail after a few minutes, stop the game and have the child move to the end of the snake to become the tail.

**Variation:**

Set up a snake racecourse on the playground. Have two or more snakes of children line up at one end of the playground. Place five or six beanbags, margarine tubs, coffee cans, or any other kind of marker in a line in front of each snake, spacing them about 5′ apart. At the starting signal, each snake must weave to the right of the first marker, to the left of the second, and so on. Each snake must make a circle around the last marker and weave back through the markers to the starting line. The first snake to return to the starting line is the winner. If a snake comes apart during the race, children must quickly get back into position before continuing.

Look carefully at the picture below.
Ten shy mice are in the picture.
Draw a circle around each mouse you find.
Then trace the dotted lines on top of the
table to see what has made the mice come
out of their hiding places.

Name _____

Name _____

Look carefully at the picture below.
Circle the three trolls who look exactly alike.
Color them exactly the same.
Then color the rest of the picture.

Read the poem on this page. Then trace the
path of each little kitten to its mittens.
Don't cross any lines.

Name _____

## THREE LITTLE KITTENS

*Three little kittens
   lost their mittens,
And they began to cry,
   "Oh, mother dear, we sadly fear,
Our mittens we have lost!"
   "What! Lost your mittens;
      you naughty kittens!
Then you shall have no pie."
   "Meow, meow, meow!"*

*The three little kittens
   found their mittens,
And they began to cry,
   "Oh, mother dear, see here, see here,
Our mittens we have found."
   "What! Found your mittens;
      you good little kittens.
Then you shall have some pie."
   "Purr, purr, purr."*

Connect the dots from 1 to 20 to see
who is making a cake in the kitchen.
Then color the picture.

Name _____

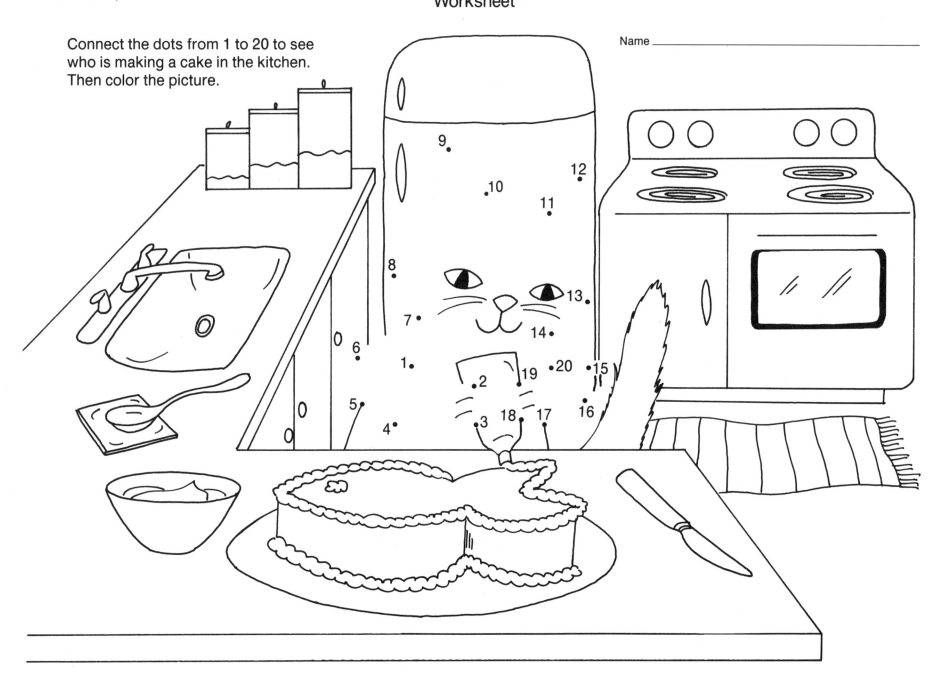

# PENCIL PLAY
## Drawing Game

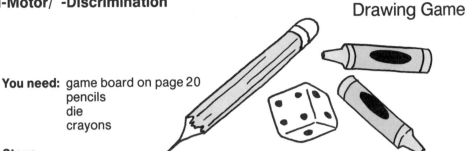

**You need:** game board on page 20
pencils
die
crayons

### Steps:

1. Groups of two to four children may play this game. Reproduce the game board on page 20 for each player. Have the players sit in a circle at a table or on the floor. Give each child a pencil.

2. Let the youngest player begin. He or she rolls the die and counts the number of dots shown on the side of the die that is faceup. With a pencil, the player then draws that number of lines between the dots on his or her game board, beginning with the dot marked "Start" and following the arrows.

3. The child to the left of the first player then takes a turn, rolling the die and drawing that number of lines connecting the dots on his or her game board.

4. The game continues in this manner until one player has connected all the dots on his or her game board and becomes the winner.

5. The other players continue taking turns until the dots on their game boards are all connected.

6. Children may then color the pictures on their game boards.

### Variations:

1. After the players have connected the dots and colored the pictures, have them glue the pictures onto oaktag. Ask each child to cut his or her picture into five large pieces, with a part of the picture showing on each piece. Have children trade their picture pieces with other players and see who can put the pieces together the fastest.

2. With younger classes, make copies of the game board on page 20 for each child. Let children simply connect the dots and color the picture.

# LITTLE FOX'S FISHING TRIP
## Maze Worksheet

Little Fox has gone fishing.
Help Little Fox find his way back to his tepee.
Little Fox's canoe cannot go past any logs.

Name _____

# HENRY'S HUNT
## Worksheet

Name _____

A durm is a very strange animal.
Henry wants to catch a durm
to give to the city zoo.
A durm's footprint looks like this:
Lead Henry to where the durm is hiding by
drawing lines to connect the durm's footprints.

# PUZZLE PLACE MATS
## Art Activity

**You need:** place-mat cutout on page 24
scissors
glue
9″ × 12″ oaktag
crayons or fine-line markers

**Optional:** clear plastic adhesive

**Steps:**

1. Make a copy of the place-mat cutout on page 24 for each child.

2. Ask children to cut out the place-mat puzzles along the dotted lines.

3. Next, have each child glue the place-mat puzzles onto the center of a 9″ × 12″ piece of oaktag. This will be the child's place mat.

4. Let children write their names on the oaktag above the puzzles. Children may then draw colorful borders around the edges of their pieces of oaktag, using crayons or fine-line markers. Ask children not to do any of the puzzles just yet.

5. Laminate each child's place mat or cover it with clear plastic adhesive.

6. Children may use crayons to do the puzzles on their place mats during snack time, or they may take them home to work on. Crayon marks may be rubbed off with an old cloth or a paper towel, and the puzzles may be done again.

Connect the dots from 1 to 20.
Then color the picture.

Trace the rabbit's path through the maze to the carrots.
Don't cross any lines.

Finish the figures below.

Draw funny faces on the heads below.

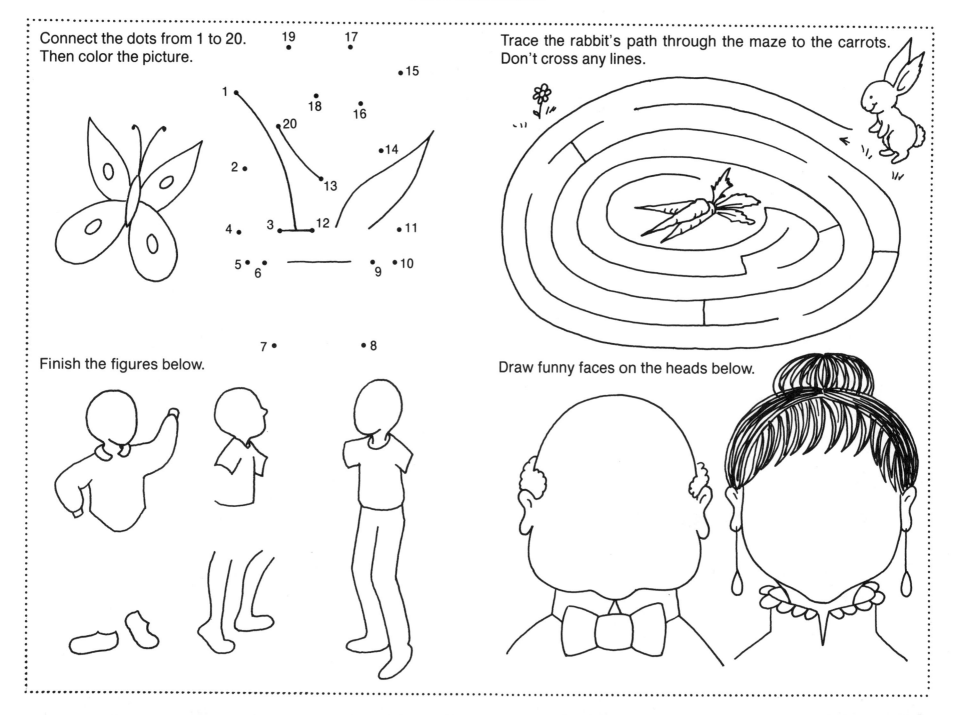

# BOATS AFLOAT
## Worksheet

Look at the boat in the first numbered box.
In the box next to it, draw shapes to make that boat look just like the boat in the first box.
Do the same with the other pairs of boats.

Name _____

Color the picture below. Cut the picture apart on the thick lines
and mix up the pieces. Then piece the puzzle together
and paste it onto a sheet of construction paper.

Name

Puzzles

**You need:** monster puzzles on this
    page and page 28
    fine-line markers
    scissors
    glue
    3″ × 5″ index cards
    manila envelope

**Optional:** clear plastic adhesive

**Steps:**

1. Reproduce the monster puzzles on this page and page 28.

2. Color the monsters with fine-line markers. Cut out and glue each puzzle onto a 3″ × 5″ index card. Laminate or cover the puzzles with clear plastic adhesive.

3. Next, cut each puzzle into two sections along the dark lines. Store the puzzle pieces in a manila envelope.

4. Let two or three children work together at a table, putting the puzzles together.

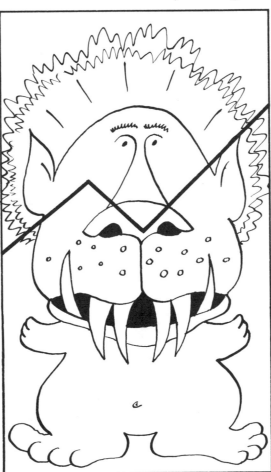

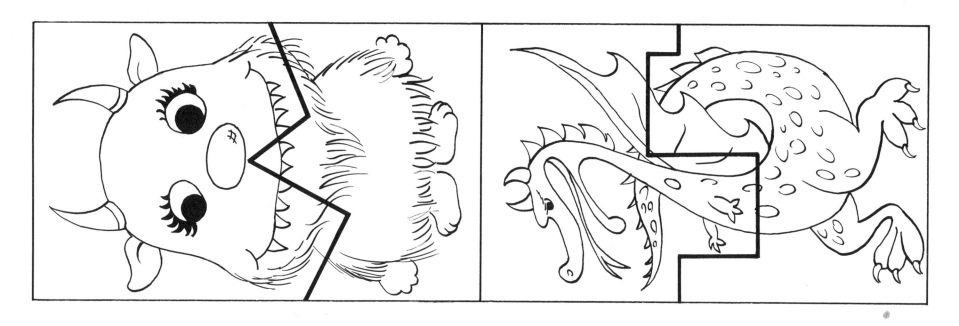

**Steps:**

1. Divide your class into groups of five or six children each.

2. Have each group sit in a circle on the floor. Ask the children to take off their shoes and place them in a pile in the center of each circle.

3. Next, have each child select from the pile two mismatched shoes that do not belong to him or her. The child places those two shoes in front of him or her.

4. When all the children have pairs of mismatched shoes in front of them, begin the game. Tell each child to pass one shoe at a time to the right, and that the object of the game is to try to be the first player to pair up his or her own shoes.

5. Each child continues to pass one shoe at a time to the player on his or her right, so that each player always has two shoes in front of him or her. When one of his or her own shoes is passed to a player, the child keeps it and passes along the other shoe. The child must stay on the lookout for the second shoe when it is passed to him or her, in order to win.

6. A player who pairs up his or her own shoes calls out, "Match up!" and becomes the winner. If desired, the winner can drop out of the game while the other players continue until all the children have matched up their shoes.

**Variation:**

Older children may play this game with sets of picture cards, letter cards, or playing cards. Make sure that the set of cards contains a different pair of matching pictures, letters, or numbers for each child in the group. Five to eight children may play this version. Have the players sit in a circle. One player shuffles the cards and deals two cards, facedown, to each of the players. Each player then picks up his or her ___ cards, looks to see what they are, and holds them in one hand s___ ___ cannot see them. If any player is dealt a match ___ ___ back to the dealer, who shuffles them ___ ___ player passes one card to th___ ___ in front of that playe___ ___ matches the one ___ ___ er may eith___ ___ er other car___ ___ nd wins the gar___ ___ ntil there is a wir___

**You need:** dark marker
16 small objects of different shapes
(block, key, plastic spoon and fork,
comb, cookie cutters, and so on)
four 9″ × 12″ pieces of oaktag
shoe box

**Steps:**

1. Use a dark marker to trace four small objects of different shapes onto a 9″ × 12″ piece of oaktag. Trace four different objects onto each of the other three pieces of oaktag. These are the four game boards.

2. Place the 16 objects into a shoe box.

3. Two to four children may play this game. Give each player a game board, and set the shoe box of objects in the center between the players.

4. Let the youngest child begin. The child closes his or her eyes, turns away from the shoe box, and picks one object out of it. The player then opens his or her eyes and tries to match the object that was picked to one of the objects that is outlined on his or her game board. If the object matches, the child places it carefully on its outline. If the object does not match, the child puts it back into the shoe box, and the child to the left of the first player takes a turn.

5. The game continues clockwise, each player in turn picking an object from the shoe box and trying to match it to an outline on his or her game board. The first player to match four objects to the four outlines on his or her game board is the winner.

**Variation:**

Adapt this game for use in an activity center. Let individual children match the objects to the outlines on all four game boards.

**You need:** scissors
four clean, empty half-pint
milk containers
3″ × 12″ strips of white
construction paper
glue
crayons or fine-line markers
picture cards on page 32
oaktag

**Steps:**

1. Cut the tops off four clean, empty half-pint milk containers.

2. Wrap a 3″ × 12″ strip of white construction paper around each container and glue in place.

3. Let several children decorate the containers to look like houses, drawing windows and doors. Children may use crayons or fine-line markers.

4. Reproduce the picture cards on page 32 four times. Mount them on oaktag and cut out. Keep each set of cards separate.

5. Teach children the traditional rhyme on this page.

6. Two to four children may play the game with the picture cards. Give each player a set of cards and a milk-carton house.

7. The players shuffle their sets of cards and lay each card facedown in a row in front of them.

8. The object of the game is to be the first player to place all eight cards in the milk-carton house. The cards must be placed in the house in the sequence of the rhyme, beginning with the malt and ending with the priest. If desired, reproduce an extra set of cards and glue them in order onto a long strip of oaktag. Children may refer to the strip of pictures to remind themselves of the rhyme's sequence.

9. The youngest player begins. He or she turns over one card. If it shows the malt, the player puts the card in the house and takes another turn, flipping over a card to see if it shows the rat. If the first card did not show the malt, the player turns the card facedown again and waits for the next turn. Players should try to remember which cards have been turned over and what they show, for future reference.

10. The game continues clockwise, each player turning over a card and placing it in the house or turning it facedown again. Each time a player puts a card in the house, he or she may take another turn. The first player to put all of his or her cards in the house is the winner.

*This is the house that Jack built.*

*This is the malt
That lay in the house that Jack built.*

*This is the rat
That ate the malt
That lay in the house that Jack built.*

*This is the cat
That killed the rat
That ate the malt
That lay in the house that Jack built.*

*This is the dog
That worried the cat
That killed the rat
That ate the malt
That lay in the house that Jack built.*

*This is the cow with the crumpled horn
That tossed the dog
That worried the cat
That killed the rat
That ate the malt
That lay in the house that Jack built.*

*This is the maiden all forlorn
That milked the cow with the crumpled horn
That tossed the dog
That worried the cat
That killed the rat
That ate the malt
That lay in the house that Jack built.*

*This is the man all tattered and torn
That kissed the maiden all forlorn
That milked the cow with the crumpled horn
That tossed the dog
That worried the cat
That killed the rat
That ate the malt
That lay in the house that Jack built.*

*This is the priest all shaven and shorn
That married the man all tattered and torn
That kissed the maiden all forlorn
That milked the cow with the crumpled horn
That tossed the dog
That worried the cat
That killed the rat
That ate the malt
That lay in the house that Jack built.*

# THE HOUSE THAT JACK BUILT
## Picture Cards

# CIRCUS FRIEND
## Puzzle

Name _____

Cut apart the five puzzle strips along the dotted lines. On another piece of paper, arrange the strips to form a picture of someone you see at the circus. Glue the strips in place and color the picture. To learn the name of your circus friend, read the letters at the left of your picture from top to bottom.

# BURIED TREASURE
## Matching Game / Game Board

**You need:** game board
glue
oaktag
scissors

**Optional:** clear plastic adhesive

**Steps:**

1. Reproduce the game board on this page eight times.

2. Glue the game boards onto oaktag. Laminate them or cover with clear plastic adhesive.

3. To make the playing cards, cut apart the pictures on four of the game boards.

4. Two to four children may play this game. Have each player take a game board.

5. Shuffle the cards and place them facedown in a single pile.

6. The object of the game is to collect all the things a pirate would have when searching for buried treasure.

7. Let the youngest player begin. He or she draws a card from the top of the pile and tries to match the card to a picture on the game board. (On their first turns, of course, the players will be able to match a picture.) If the card matches, the player covers the picture with the matching card; if the player has already covered the picture on his or her game board, the card is placed facedown on the bottom of the pile.

8. The game continues clockwise, each player drawing one card and trying to match it to a picture on his or her game board.

9. The first player to cover all nine pictures on the game board calls out, "Yo-ho-ho! The buried treasure is mine!" and becomes the winner.

# FIDO'S SURPRISE
## Make a Minibook

Name _____

Oscar is making something to surprise his dog, Fido.
Color and cut out the six pictures below.
Write numbers from 1 to 6 in the circles.
Then put the pictures in order and staple them together
to make a minibook.

# STAR PUZZLERS
### Letter-Matching Activity / Pattern

**You need:** star pattern
scissors
pencil
six different colors of oaktag
dark marker
large envelope

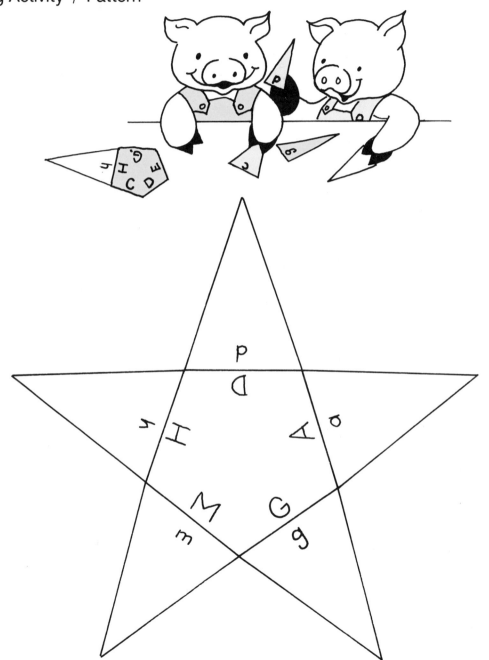

### Steps:

1. Reproduce the star pattern on this page and cut out.

2. Trace the star pattern once onto each color of oaktag. Then cut out the six stars and cut off the points of each one.

3. With a dark marker, write five different uppercase letters on the sides of a star center, one in the middle of each edge, as shown. Then write the corresponding lowercase letters at the bases of five star points of a matching color.

4. Do the same with the remaining star centers and points. (Four letters of the alphabet will be repeated.)

5. Place the star centers and points in a large envelope.

6. In their free time, one or two children may piece together these puzzles, matching the lowercase letters to their uppercase counterparts.

### Variations:

1. To make this a counting activity, substitute numerals for the upper-case letters and draw corresponding numbers of dots on the star points.

2. Have younger children match identical pictures. Draw simple figures or shapes on the star centers and matching ones on the star points.

3. To make this a flannel-board activity, attach a small piece of felt or flannel to the back of each puzzle piece. Have children put the star centers on the flannel board and then place the star points in the correct places.

# LETTER LAUNCH
Worksheet

Look for the different letters in this puzzle.

Name _____

Find the *R*s.
Color the spaces red.

Find the *B*s.
Color the spaces blue.

Find the *Y*s.
Color the spaces yellow.

Find the *G*s.
Color the spaces green.

Find the *P*s.
Color the spaces purple.

Find the *O*s.
Color the spaces orange.

What do you see? _____

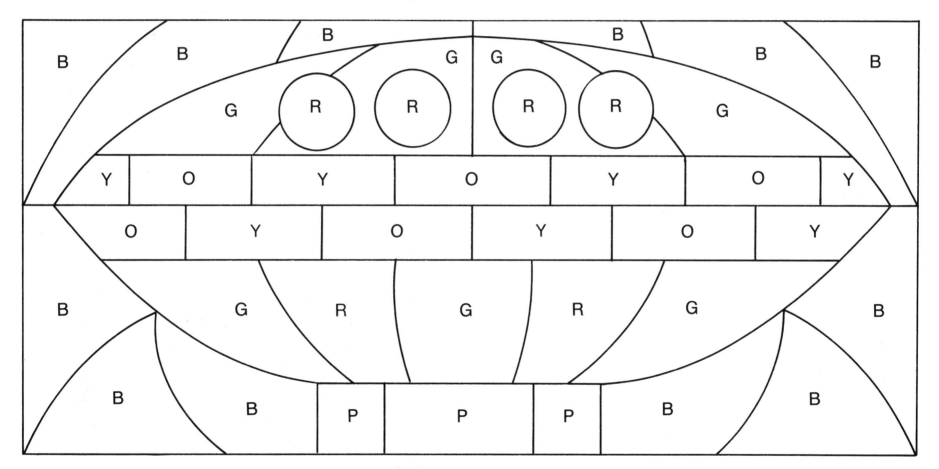

**You need:** 3″ × 5″ unlined index cards
fine-line markers or crayons
paper clips
brown-paper grocery bag

## Steps:

1. Give each child one 3″ × 5″ unlined index card for each letter in his or her first name.

2. Ask children to write their names on the cards, one letter per card, with fine-line markers or crayons.

3. Let children decorate each of their letter cards with silly drawings and interesting designs.

4. When children have finished decorating their cards, ask each child to scramble the letters of his or her name and then put the cards together in a pile.

5. Collect each child's pile of cards and secure them with a paper clip.

6. Put the children's name cards in a brown-paper grocery bag. Let each child draw one bundle of someone else's cards from the bag.

7. Each child will unscramble the name of a classmate, laying the letter cards in order on his or her desk.

8. When a child has successfully unscrambled the classmate's name, he or she will return the cards to that child.

## Variation:

Have children bring photographs of themselves from home, or have them draw self-portraits. Post children's pictures on a bulletin board. Write each child's name on a strip of white paper and pin it below his or her picture. Below that strip of paper, pin the letters of the student's name, scrambled. Then let children work together to unscramble everyone's name.

**You need:** scissors
plastic-foam egg carton
dark marker
egg pictures on this page
glue
oaktag

Step 4.

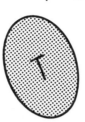

**Steps:**

1. Cut the bottom section of the egg carton in half lengthwise to form two rows of six cups each.

2. With a dark marker, print these letters on the fronts of the egg-carton cups in each row: T, G, N, P, D, K.

3. Make two copies of the egg pictures on this page. Glue the pictures onto oaktag and cut out.

4. On the back of each egg, write the picture's ending sound.

5. Put a set of egg pictures near each row of egg-carton cups. In their free time, one or two children may sort the egg pictures into the egg-carton cups, matching the ending sounds of the pictured objects with the letters marked on the egg-carton cups. Children may check their work by turning over each egg picture to see the correct ending-sound letter.

**Variation:**

Make this a beginning-sounds game. Cut out pictures from discarded reading-readiness workbooks and glue them onto egg-shaped pieces of oaktag. On the back of each egg picture, write the beginning-sound letter. Then label the egg-carton cups with the appropriate letters.

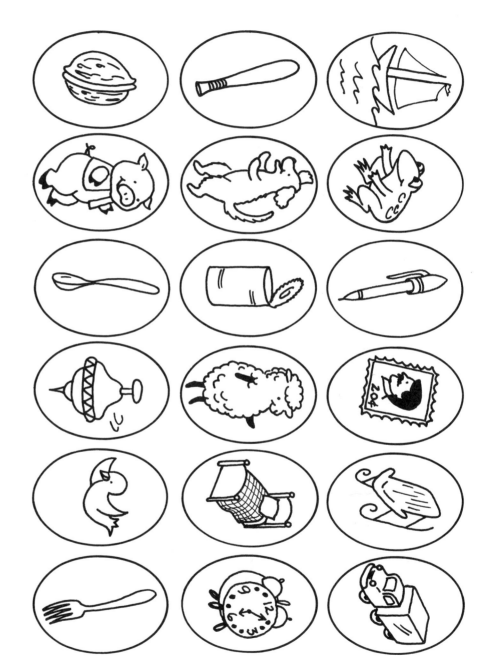

# NOISY ANIMALS
## Crossword Puzzle

Read the crossword clues and fill in the correct words in the puzzle. Use the word bank for extra help.

Name _____

### Word Bank

| | |
|---|---|
| pig | horse |
| dog | sheep |
| hen | cow |
| duck | turkey |

## DOWN

1. This animal has many large feathers and says "Gobble!"

2. This animal is woolly and says "Baa!"

3. This animal lays eggs and says "Cluck!"

4. This animal wags its tail and says "Bow-wow!"

5. This animal gives us milk and says "Moo!"

## ACROSS

3. This animal eats hay and says "Neigh!"

4. This animal has webbed feet and says "Quack!"

6. This animal has a curly tail and says "Oink!"

**You need:** game board on page 42
glue
oaktag
pumpkin pattern on this page
scissors
pencil
9″ × 12″ orange oaktag
dark marker
3″ × 5″ unlined index cards

**Steps:**

1. Two to four children may play this game. Reproduce the game board on page 42 for each player and glue each one onto oaktag.

2. Next, make a copy of the pumpkin pattern on this page and cut out. Trace the pumpkin onto orange oaktag, making seven for each player, and cut out the pumpkins.

3. With a dark marker, write a different reading word on each pumpkin. Use words the children are learning now—if possible, words that have similar letter combinations, such as *his* and *has*, *car* and *cat*, and *was* and *saw*.

4. Then write each of the words that appears on the pumpkins on separate 3″ × 5″ unlined index cards.

5. Have the players sit side by side at a table, and give each player a game board. Each player selects seven pumpkins and places them word-side down on the dotted outlines on his or her game board. (The object of the game is to remove these pumpkins from the game board.) Players may look at the words on the pumpkins before putting them in place.

6. One player shuffles the index cards and places them facedown in a pile in front of the players.

7. The youngest player goes first, turning over the top index card. All the players look at the word for five to ten seconds before the first player turns the card facedown again. All players then begin turning over the pumpkins on their game boards, trying to find the word that matches the one written on the card.

8. A player who thinks he or she has found the pumpkin with the matching word compares it with the card that was turned over. If the words match, the player keeps the pumpkin off the board, and the word card is removed from the pile. If the word does not match, the player puts the pumpkin back on the game board facedown and puts the card facedown on the bottom of the pile. Players then check to see that all the pumpkins on the game boards are turned facedown before continuing the game.

9. Players take turns flipping over the word cards one at a time, studying each one for a few seconds before turning it facedown again, and then checking their pumpkins for the matching words. The first player to remove all the pumpkins from his or her game board is the winner.

**Variations:**

1. For younger children, make this a letter-matching game by substituting letters for the words on the pumpkins and cards.

2. Pairs of children can play a spelling game with the pumpkins and game boards. Write 14 different spelling words on the cards and place them facedown in a pile. Each player takes a game board and seven pumpkins. One player takes a card and reads it to the other player, who must spell the word. If the player spells the word correctly, he or she puts a pumpkin on his or her game board. If the word is misspelled, the player does nothing and the card is turned facedown and placed on the bottom of the pile. Players alternate turns, one reading a word and the other spelling it. The first player to fill all the spaces on his or her game board with pumpkins is the winner.

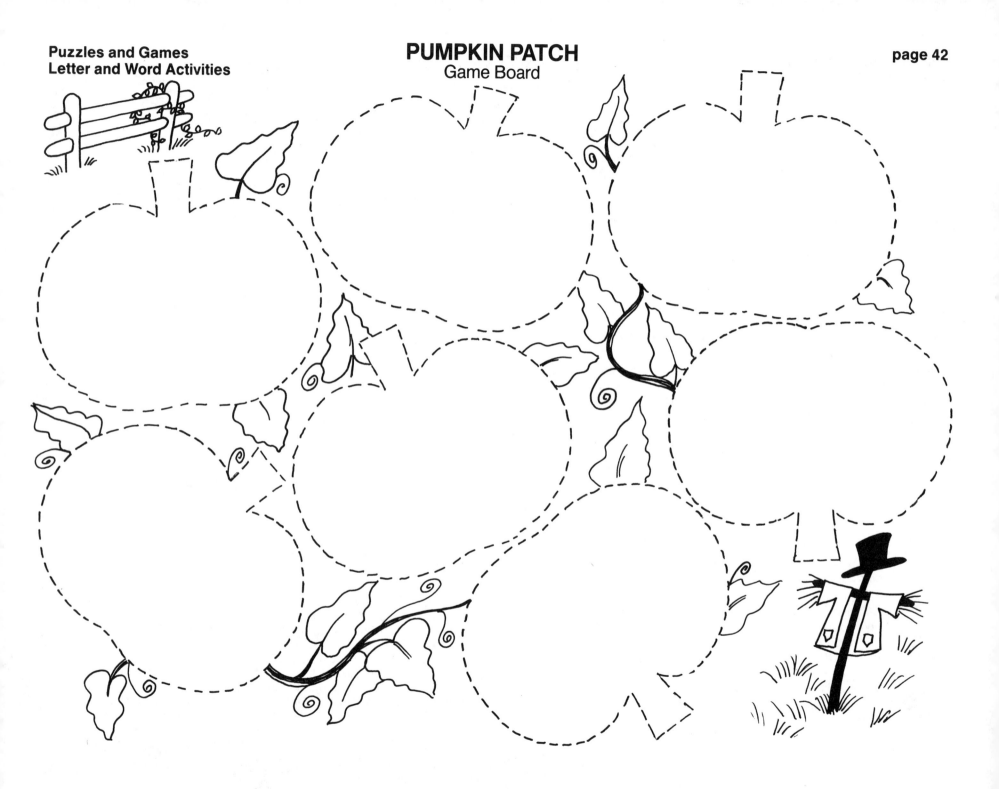

In the word puzzle, find the baseball words listed in the Word Bank. The words may be written from top to bottom or from left to right. Some words may share some letters. One word has been circled for you.

Name _____

| Word Bank | | |
|------|------|------|
| bat | catch | mitt |
| ball | base | run |
| cap | hit | out |
| walk | safe | pitch |

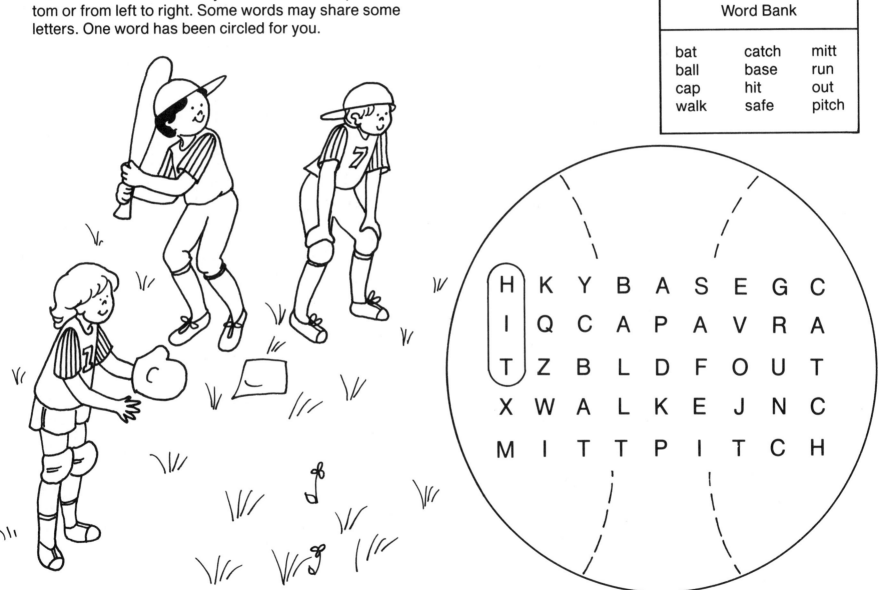

# ANIMAL RIDDLES
### Worksheet

Read the riddles below. To solve them, look at the numeral below each blank space. Check the key to find the letter that goes with each numeral. Write the letters in the blank spaces and read the answers to the riddles.

Name _____

| KEY | | |
|---|---|---|
| 1=M | 10=V | 19=E |
| 2=N | 11=W | 20=F |
| 3=O | 12=X | 21=G |
| 4=P | 13=Y | 22=H |
| 5=Q | 14=Z | 23=I |
| 6=R | 15=A | 24=J |
| 7=S | 16=B | 25=K |
| 8=T | 17=C | 26=L |
| 9=U | 18=D | |

1. Which animal keeps time?

$\overline{15}$  $\overline{11}$  $\overline{15}$  $\overline{8}$  $\overline{17}$  $\overline{22}$   $\overline{18}$  $\overline{3}$  $\overline{21}$

2. Which animal do you use to measure?

$\overline{15}$  $\overline{2}$   $\overline{23}$  $\overline{2}$  $\overline{17}$  $\overline{22}$  $\overline{11}$  $\overline{3}$  $\overline{6}$  $\overline{1}$

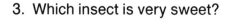

3. Which insect is very sweet?

$\overline{15}$   $\overline{22}$  $\overline{3}$  $\overline{2}$  $\overline{19}$  $\overline{13}$  $\overline{16}$  $\overline{19}$  $\overline{19}$

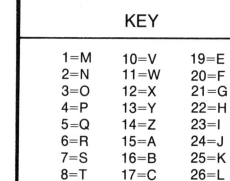

4. What does a pig use to write a letter with?

$\overline{15}$   $\overline{4}$  $\overline{23}$  $\overline{21}$  $\overline{4}$  $\overline{19}$  $\overline{2}$

5. Which bird is always sad?

$\overline{15}$   $\overline{16}$  $\overline{26}$  $\overline{9}$  $\overline{19}$  $\overline{16}$  $\overline{23}$  $\overline{6}$  $\overline{18}$

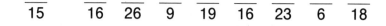
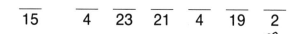

# DECODE THE CLUES
## Code Game / Code Wheel

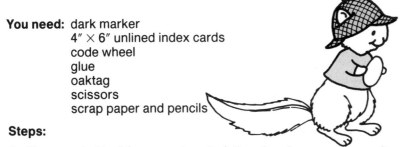

**You need:** dark marker
4″ × 6″ unlined index cards
code wheel
glue
oaktag
scissors
scrap paper and pencils

### Steps:

1. Plan a coded trail for your class to follow. In advance, prepare five or six short clues that tell children where to look for the next clues. With a dark marker, write each clue (except the first clue) on a 4″ × 6″ unlined index card, using the code shown on the code wheel. Some examples:

   behind door— □/●/○●○/■/○■○/◡  ◡/◡/◡/◡◡

   on table— ◡/○■○  □□/○/□/○◡●/●

   near clock— ○■○/●/○/◡◡◡  ○□/○◡●/◡/○□/□●□

   next to window— ○■○/●/◡◡/□□  □□/◡
   ■■■/■/○■○/◡/◡◡/■■■

   on top of bookcase— ◡/○■○  □□/◡/◡■○  ◡/●□
   □/◡/◡/□●□/○□/○/○◡/●

   Place these clues in appropriate places around the room before children come to class. Prepare this coded phrase as the final message:

   You are a good decoder.— ●●●/◡/●●  ○/◡◡◡/●  ○
   □◡/◡/◡/◡  ◡/●/○□/◡/◡/●/◡◡◡

2. Reproduce the code wheel on this page for each child. Have each child glue the code wheel onto oaktag and cut out.

3. Next, practice decoding a few simple words with the children. Write such words as *yes*, *here*, *by*, and *girl* on the chalkboard in code and show children how to use the code wheels to decode the words.

4. Give each child some scrap paper and a pencil. Divide the class into teams of two or three children each.

5. Write the first clue on the chalkboard. The teams of children will copy it on their papers, work together to decode it, and follow its directions. Children will do the same for each coded message.

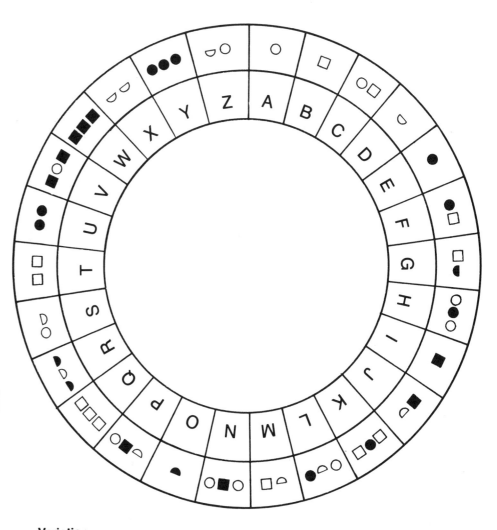

### Variation:

In their free time, children may use their code wheels to help write coded messages for their classmates to decode.

### Follow-up Activity:

Reproduce the worksheet on page 46 for each child. Have children use their code wheels to find out what is happening in the story.

Name _____

Use the code wheel (page 45) to find
out what is happening in the pictures below.
On the lines at the bottom of each picture,
write the decoded sentence.

The six boxes on this page tell the story of a Martian. The story is written in Martian. Use the Letter Key to decode the Martian words. Write the words in English on the lines in each box. Then cut out the boxes and staple them together to make a minibook.

Letter Key

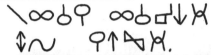

| | | | | | | |
|---|---|---|---|---|---|---|
| A= ↑ | E= ↓ | I= ꝺ | M= ♀ | Q= ⊙ | U= ▯ | X= ⧓ |
| B= / | F= ⏋ | J= ⌐ | N= ∿ | R= ◁ | V= ⬓ | Y= Ⴑ |
| C= O | G= \ | K= ✳ | O= ↕ | S= ⋈ | W= 8 | Z= > |
| D= △ | H= □ | L= ∞ | P= ⊖ | T= < | | |

1. _____

2. _____

3. _____

4. _____

5. _____

6. _____

**You need:** 5″ × 8″ unlined index cards
dark markers
thumbtacks or pushpins
shoe box
assortment of small objects: paper
clips, dried beans and seeds,
toothpicks, buttons, macaroni,
and so on
glue

### Steps:

1. On ten 5″ × 8″ unlined index cards, write the numerals 1 to 10. Use a dark marker and make the numerals large.

2. Pin the cards in numerical order near the top of a bulletin board, leaving space below each card where other cards may be pinned.

3. Now write three more sets of the numerals 1 to 10 and distribute one or more cards to each child in your class.

4. Fill a shoe box with an assortment of small objects, such as paper clips, dried beans and seeds, toothpicks, buttons, and macaroni.

5. Ask children to look at the numeral written on each of their cards. They will glue that number of one object onto the other side of each card.

6. When the glue has dried, collect the cards, check to see that the correct number of objects is on each one, and place them object-side up on a table near the bulletin board.

7. Let two or three children work together, pinning all the cards holding objects below the corresponding numeral cards on the bulletin board. They may check under each card to see if the numeral on the back matches the numeral card on the board. When one group has finished, remove all the cards so that another group may pin them on the bulletin board.

# SPOTTED SEA MONSTER
## Counting Puzzle / Patterns

**You need:** sea monster patterns
scissors
pencil
yellow oaktag
colored markers

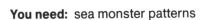
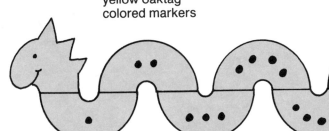

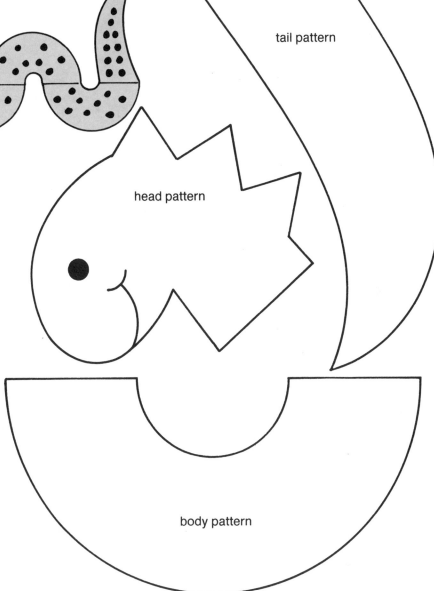

tail pattern

head pattern

body pattern

### Steps:

1. Reproduce the sea monster patterns on this page. Cut them out, and trace the head and tail patterns once onto yellow oaktag. Then trace the body pattern nine times onto yellow oaktag.

2. Cut out all the body parts. Use colored markers to draw facial features on the monster's head.

3. Next, draw colored dots on the nine body parts—one dot on the first part, two on the second, and so on. Use a variety of colors. Draw ten dots on the monster's tail.

4. Let individual children piece the spotted sea monster together, beginning by connecting the section with one dot to the head and adding on the remaining sections in sequence from two dots to ten.

### Variation:

To help children practice alphabetical order, make 25 body sections for the sea monster. Write an uppercase letter on the left-hand side of each section and the corresponding lowercase letter on the right-hand side. Label the tail section with a capital and lowercase *z*. Turn alternate sections upside down as you write the letters, so that all the letters will be right-side up when the sea monster is pieced together.

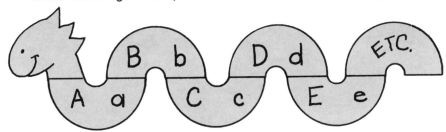

Cut out the license plates at the right-hand side of this page.
Solve the addition problem on each license plate and paste it
onto the race car with the matching sum on its side.

Name _____

7 + 3 =

8 + 7 =

12 + 6 =

6 + 8 =

5 + 11 =

7 + 5 =

14 + 5 =

9 + 4 =

13 + 4 =

# HAUNTED HOUSE
## Math Worksheet

Name _____

Look at the haunted house on this page.
Then fill in the chart below.
In the row beginning with the picture of a bat,
color in one space for each bat that is haunting the house.
Fill in the other rows in the chart, coloring in one space
for each creature that is haunting the house.
Then use the chart to help you answer the questions at
the bottom of the page.

| How many . . . ? | 1 | 2 | 3 | 4 | 5 |
|---|---|---|---|---|---|
| 🦇 |  |  |  |  |  |
| 🧙 |  |  |  |  |  |
| 🐈 |  |  |  |  |  |
| 👻 |  |  |  |  |  |

1. How many bats are there? _____

2. How many cats are there? _____

3. How many ghosts and witches are there? _____

4. How many more bats are there than witches? _____

5. How many more cats are there than ghosts? _____

# SANTA'S HELPERS
## Math Worksheet

Hup, Num, Mot, Rab, and Pok are elves who work for Santa.
The chart on this page shows how many toys each elf made in one day.
Use the chart and the key to answer the questions at the bottom of the page.

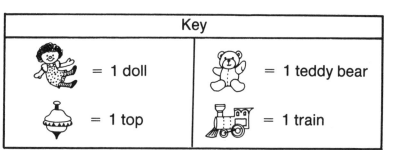

Name _____

| Key | | | |
|---|---|---|---|
| | = 1 doll | | = 1 teddy bear |
| | = 1 top | | = 1 train |

| Hup | Num | Mot | Rab | Pok |
|---|---|---|---|---|

1. How many trains did Num make? _____

2. How many teddy bears did Rab make? _____    4. How many tops were made in all? _____

3. Who made the most dolls? _____    5. Who made the most toys? _____

# PLAYGROUND PALS
## Worksheet

Cut out the eight pictures at the bottom of the page. Read the names of the two animals in the first box. Paste their pictures in the squares on the seesaw, putting the heavier animal in the lower square and the lighter animal in the higher square. Do the same in each of the other boxes. Can you tell why the twin rabbits are at the same height on the seesaw in the last box?

Name _____

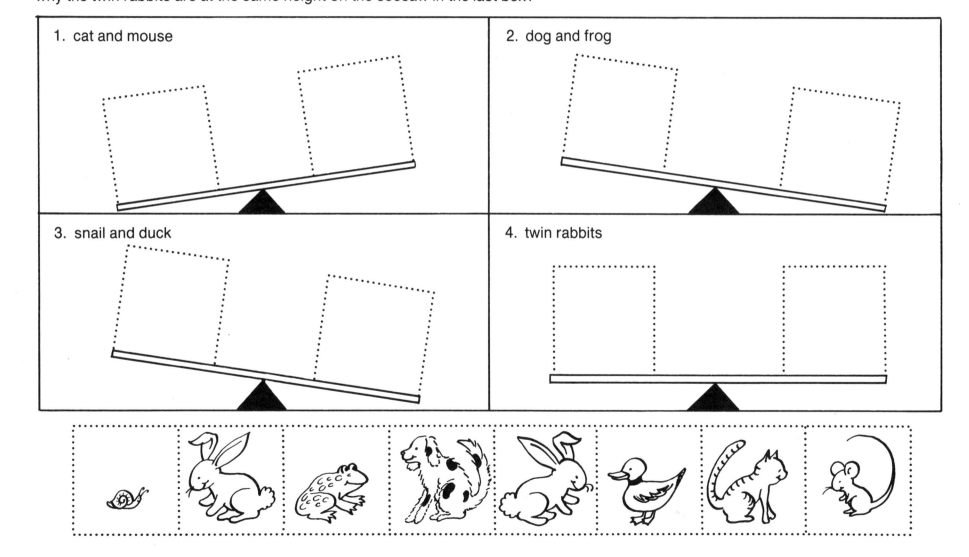

1. cat and mouse

2. dog and frog

3. snail and duck

4. twin rabbits

**You need:** two 12″ × 18″ pieces of oaktag
ruler
pencil
scissors
dark marker
insect cards
glue

**Steps:**

1. On a 12″ × 18″ piece of oaktag, measure and draw a square 10″ on each side. Cut out the square.

2. On the square, use a pencil to mark off a grid containing five rows of five small squares. Each side of the small squares should measure 2″. Trace over the lines of the grid with a dark marker.

3. Next, make five copies of the insect cards on this page. Glue the cards onto oaktag and cut out.

4. Remove four of the five bee cards and any two other cards from the deck and set them aside. Only the 24 remaining cards are needed for the game.

5. Two, three, or four children may play this game. One player shuffles the insect cards and places them facedown in the squares of the grid, leaving the center square empty.

6. The object of the game is for each player to catch as many insects as possible. To catch an insect, a player "jumps" over one card by moving an adjacent card up, down, to the right or to the left, and into an empty square. Diagonal jumps are not allowed. The card that was jumped is turned faceup. If it shows the bee, the player gets "stung" and does not catch an insect on that turn. The bee card is turned facedown again in the same square. If the card that was jumped shows any other insect, the player keeps the card. Any card may be used to jump over another card, as long as the two cards are next to each other and there is an empty square on the other side of the card being jumped. Once the bee card has been turned facedown again, children should try to keep track of it to avoid being stung.

7. Let the youngest child begin. He or she jumps one card over another into the center square and checks to see which insect is on the card that was jumped. The child to the left of the first player then takes a turn. The game continues clockwise, each player making one jump per turn.

8. When players can no longer take turns because none of the cards remaining on the grid are next to each other, each player counts the insects he or she has caught. The player with the most insects is the winner. In the case of a tie, the game is a draw.

**Variations:**

1. One child may play a solitaire version of this game. The child shuffles the 24 cards and lays them facedown on the grid, leaving the center square empty. He or she then jumps one card over another, removing cards and trying to catch as many insects as possible. The game ends when no more cards can be jumped. The child may play the game several times, each time trying to improve his or her score.

2. Groups of two to four children can use the insect cards to play a memory game. Prepare a deck containing four cards of each type of insect. One player shuffles the cards and lays them facedown on a table or floor in four rows of six cards each. The first player turns over any two cards; if they match, the player keeps the cards. If the cards don't match, they are turned facedown again. The players take turns, each flipping over two cards to see if they match. Children should try to remember where the unmatched cards are for future turns. When all the cards have been matched, the player who has the most pairs of cards is the winner.

# NUTTY SQUIRRELS
## Guessing Game

**You need:** game boards on page 56
glue
oaktag
scissors
red and brown crayons
manila folders
old cloth or paper towels

**Optional:** clear plastic adhesive

**Steps:**

1. If you would like your students to practice letter recognition, use the lettered game board on page 56. To have children review numbers, use the numbered game board on page 56. Make a copy of the appropriate game board for each player.

2. Glue the game boards onto oaktag and cut them out. Laminate them or cover with clear plastic adhesive.

3. Pairs of children may play this game. Each player gets a game board and a red and a brown crayon.

4. Open a manila folder and stand it up between the two players so that it screens each player's game board from the other player's view.

5. Each player pretends that he or she is a squirrel who has hidden four nuts on his or her game board. Four brown **X**'s are marked on the board to represent the nuts.

6. The younger player begins by asking, "Did you hide a nut on the A [or 1, or any other letter or number on the game board] square?" The other player must answer "yes" or "no." If the answer is "yes," both players draw red circles around that square on their game boards. If the answer is "no," the first player marks that square with a red **X**.

7. Players alternate turns, naming lettered or numbered squares where they think their opponents may have hidden nuts. The first player to locate all four of them is the winner.

8. Have children wipe their game boards clean with an old cloth or a paper towel after each game.

| A | B | C | D | E |
|---|---|---|---|---|
| F | G | H | I | J |
| K | L | M | N | O |
| P | Q | R | S | T |
| U | V | W | X | Y |

Z

| 1 | 2 | 3 | 4 | 5 |
|---|---|---|---|---|
| 6 | 7 | 8 | 9 | 10 |
| 11 | 12 | 13 | 14 | 15 |
| 16 | 17 | 18 | 19 | 20 |
| 21 | 22 | 23 | 24 | 25 |

# TROLL TROUBLE
## Strategy Game

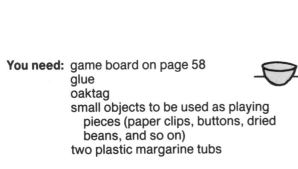

**You need:** game board on page 58
glue
oaktag
small objects to be used as playing
    pieces (paper clips, buttons, dried
    beans, and so on)
two plastic margarine tubs

**Steps:**

1. Reproduce the game board on page 58 and glue it onto oaktag.

2. Place 16 small objects of the same sort in one plastic margarine tub. In the other margarine tub, place 16 small objects of a different sort.

3. Two children may play this game. Each player takes a margarine tub of playing pieces.

4. The object of the game is to <u>avoid</u> being the player to land on the last space at the bottom of the mountain. A troublesome troll is waiting there to capture the first person to reach the bottom of the mountain.

5. The youngest player goes first. He or she begins at the top of the mountain and places one, two, or three playing pieces in consecutive spaces on the trail, one playing piece per space.

6. The other player then takes a turn, placing from one to three of his or her playing pieces on the trail, beginning with the first empty space.

7. Players alternate turns. As each player nears the end of the trail, he or she must choose carefully how many playing pieces to use so that his or her opponent lands on the last space, where the troll is waiting.

8. Have children play five rounds of this game, taking turns being the first player. The player who wins the most rounds is the champ.

9. If desired, prepare additional game boards and margarine tubs of playing pieces so that several pairs of children can play this game at once.

**Variation:**

Older children may play this game in groups of three. Give each player 12 playing pieces of the same sort. During their turns, players may place one or two playing pieces on the trail.

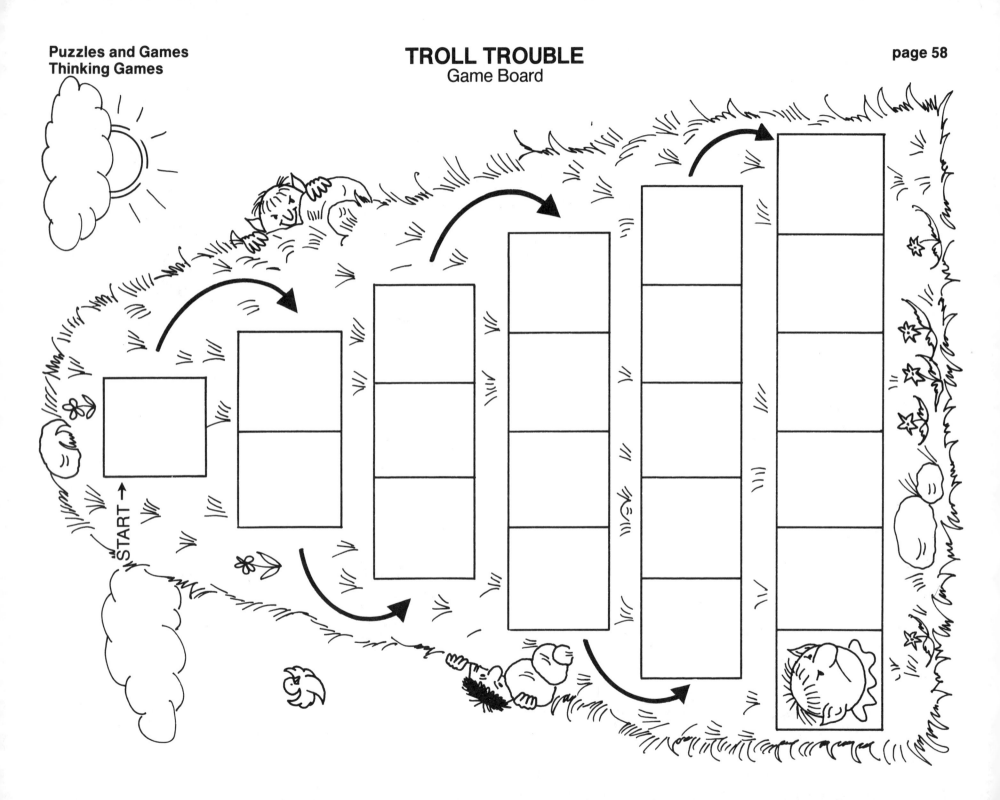

**Boats Afloat**
**(page 25)**

1. add second smokestack and third porthole

2. add right sail and crow's nest

3. add life preserver and flag

4. add second smokestack and stripes on side of boat

5. add periscope and propeller

6. add anchor and ladder

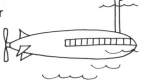

**Batter Up!**
**(page 43)**

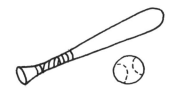

| H | K | Y | B | A | S | E | G | C |
|---|---|---|---|---|---|---|---|---|
| I | Q | C | A | P | A | V | R | A |
| T | Z | B | L | D | F | O | U | T |
| X | W | A | L | K | E | J | N | C |
| M | I | T | T | P | I | T | C | H |

**Noisy Animals**
**(page 40)**

### Animal Riddles
### (page 44)

1. <u>A</u> <u>W</u> <u>A</u> <u>T</u> <u>C</u> <u>H</u>   <u>D</u> <u>O</u> <u>G</u>
   15   11   15   8   17   22    18   3   21

2. <u>A</u> <u>N</u>   <u>I</u> <u>N</u> <u>C</u> <u>H</u> <u>W</u> <u>O</u> <u>R</u> <u>M</u>
   15   2    23   2   17   22   11   3   6   1

3. <u>A</u>   <u>H</u> <u>O</u> <u>N</u> <u>E</u> <u>Y</u> <u>B</u> <u>E</u> <u>E</u>
   15    22   3   2   19   13   16   19   19

4. <u>A</u>   <u>P</u> <u>I</u> <u>G</u> <u>P</u> <u>E</u> <u>N</u>
   15    4   23   21   4   19   2

5. <u>A</u>   <u>B</u> <u>L</u> <u>U</u> <u>E</u> <u>B</u> <u>I</u> <u>R</u> <u>D</u>
   15    16   26   9   19   16   23   6   18

### Alice's Hat
### (page 46)

1. Alice lost her new hat.
2. A bird found Alice's hat.
3. The bird hung the hat in a tree.
4. Now Alice's hat is the bird's nest.

### Martian Minibook
### (page 47)

1. This is Glim.
2. Glim lives on Mars.
3. Glim flies a spaceship.
4. Glim likes to fly quickly.
5. Glim likes to fly low.
6. Glim likes to fly in loops.

### Race-Car Math
### (page 50)

Car 15 = 8 + 7

Car 16 = 5 + 11

Car 12 = 7 + 5

Car 14 = 6 + 8

Car 19 = 14 + 5

Car 10 = 7 + 3

Car 18 = 12 + 6

Car 13 = 9 + 4

Car 17 = 13 + 4

### Haunted House
### (page 51)

1. five

2. four

3. five

4. three

5. one

### Santa's Helpers
### (page 52)

1. three

2. three

3. Rab

4. sixteen

5. Mot

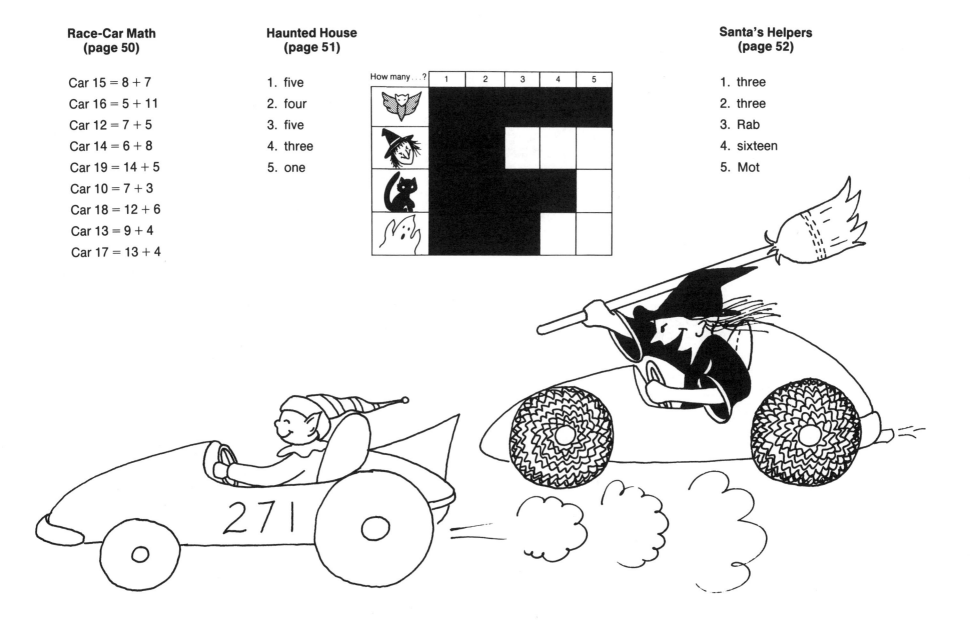

**You need:** scissors
crayons or markers
game board, spinner, and
  playing pieces (see below)
glue
oaktag
sharpened pencil

**Optional:** clear plastic adhesive

### To Prepare the Game:

1. Draw a castle in the center of a large sheet of paper. The paper should be big enough for children to use as a game board. Then draw a zigzagging path leading to the castle. Make sure that you have obvious starting and ending points. Section the path into squares, like those on a traditional game board, on which the playing pieces will be moved.

2. Within each square, draw a colored shape: a purple circle, yellow star, green triangle, blue square, orange rectangle, and red heart. Glue the game board to oaktag for sturdiness. Laminate or cover with clear plastic adhesive.

3. To make the spinner, cut out a hexagon, and divide it into six sections. In each section, draw one of the colored shapes listed in Step 2. Then poke a sharpened pencil through the center hole and push the hexagon three-quarters of the way up the pencil, with the colored shapes facing away from the pencil's point.

4. To make playing pieces, invite children to draw a fairy-tale character, such as a knight, a king, a prince, a queen, or a princess, on a small rectangle of oaktag. Help cut a slit at the bottom of the figure, then cut out a smaller oaktag rectangle. Slip the small rectangle into the slit. (See illustration above.)

### How to Play:

*For younger children:*

1. This version of the game reinforces children's recognition of different colors and shapes. Two to six children may play. Each player selects a knight and places it on the space marked "Start."

2. The youngest child takes the first turn. He or she spins the pencil on its point. The spinner will fall to rest on one of its six sides, showing a colored shape. The player must move his or her knight forward to the nearest space on the game board showing that colored shape.

3. Play continues clockwise, each player spinning the spinner and moving his or her knight forward along the trail to the castle.

4. To capture the castle, a player must spin the spinner and move to the square inside the castle that shows the same colored shape. The first player to capture the castle is the winner.

*For older children:*

1. This version of the game helps children practice simple addition and subtraction. Two to six children may play.

2. Reproduce the playing cards on pages 63 and 64. Mount them on oaktag and laminate or cover with clear plastic adhesive. Then cut out the cards, shuffle them, and place them facedown in a pile next to the game board.

3. Have each player choose a knight and place it on the space marked "Start."

4. The youngest player begins. He or she takes a card from the top of the pile, reads the math problem aloud, and gives the answer. If the answer is correct, the player moves his or her knight that number of spaces ahead on the game board. If the answer is incorrect or if the answer is zero, the player loses his or her turn. The card is then placed faceup beside the pile of cards.

5. Play continues clockwise, each student selecting a card, solving the problem, and moving his or her knight along the trail.

6. When all the cards have been used, shuffle them and turn them facedown again.

7. The first player to enter the castle and capture it is the winner. A player captures the castle by solving a problem whose answer is <u>greater</u> than the number of spaces between the player's knight and the castle.

### Variations:

1. Young children may practice counting skills by rolling a die and moving their playing pieces the corresponding number of spaces.

2. For older children, prepare a set of 24 or more spelling-word cards to use with the game. Write the spelling words on separate 3″ × 5″ unlined index cards and place the cards facedown in a pile next to the game board. One player draws a card from the top of the pile and reads the word to the player on his or her left. That child must spell the word. If the player spells the word correctly, he or she moves his or her knight the number of letters in the word. The game continues in this manner until one child captures the castle by correctly spelling a word with more letters than the number of spaces between the player's knight and the castle.

| | | | | | |
|---|---|---|---|---|---|
| 6 − 1 = | 5 − 1 = | 4 − 4 = | 3 − 2 = | 2 − 1 = | 1 − 1 = |
| 2 + 3 = | 3 + 3 = | 4 + 2 = | 2 + 1 = | 4 + 1 = | 1 + 1 = |
| 9 − 3 = | 8 − 3 = | 7 − 4 = | 5 − 2 = | 6 − 4 = | 7 − 5 = |
| 4 + 4 = | 5 + 2 = | 3 + 1 = | 1 + 5 = | 3 + 4 = | 0 + 2 = |

| $11 - 11 =$ | $10 - 6 =$ | $12 - 9 =$ | $14 - 11 =$ | $15 - 10 =$ | $10 - 5 =$ |

| $0 + 6 =$ | $2 + 2 =$ | $3 + 0 =$ | $6 + 1 =$ | $5 + 3 =$ | $2 + 8 =$ |

| $14 - 9 =$ | $13 - 8 =$ | $16 - 12 =$ | $10 - 8 =$ | $7 - 7 =$ | $11 - 6 =$ |

| $3 + 7 =$ | $12 - 6 =$ | $4 + 5 =$ | $9 - 7 =$ | $6 + 2 =$ | $15 - 12 =$ |